WITHDRAWN

DATE DUE

A POCKETFUL OF
PYTHON

PICKED
BY
JOHN
CLEESE

WITH A PREFACE BY MICHAEL PALIN

methuen

WRITTEN AND CONCEIVED BY GRAHAM CHAPMAN, JOHN CLEESE TERRY GILLIAM, ERIC IDLE TERRY JONES AND MICHAEL PALIN

DESIGN BY KATY HEPBURN AND ALUN EVANS

Special thanks to Bristol Zoo, Jersey Zoo, London Zoo and Marwell Zoo
for photographs of Lemurs
Back flap Lemur photograph courtesy of Telegraph Picture Library
'Last Supper' illustration by Pearce Marchbank
Co-ordinating editor for the *Pocketful of Python* series: Geoffrey Strachan

The texts included in this volume are taken from the TV scripts for *Monty
Python's Flying Circus*, published by Methuen in 1989 as *Monty Python's Flying
Circus: Just the Words*; the film screenplays for *Monty Python and the Holy
Grail, The Life of Brian* and *The Meaning of Life*, published by Methuen in 1977,
1979, and 1983; *The Brand New Monty Python Bok*, published in paperback as
The Brand New Monty Python Papperbok (Methuen 1973 and 1974); *The Fairly
Incomplete and Rather Badly Illustrated Monty Python Song Book* (1994) and the
record album/CD *The Monty Python Matching Tie and Handkerchief* (1975)

Published by Methuen 1999
3 5 7 9 10 8 6 4 2

First published in Great Britain by
Methuen Publishing Limited, 215 Vauxhall Bridge Road, London SW1V 1EJ

Methuen Publishing Limited Reg. No 3543167
A CIP catalogue record for this title is available from the British Library

ISBN 0 413 74160 5
Printed and bound in Great Britain by Butler and Tanner Ltd, Frome, Somerset

It is indeed an honour to be able to pen a few words by way of introduction to John's selection of Python literary memorabilia. Well, quite an honour. Actually, it's a bit of a bloody nuisance as I'd hoped to have the afternoon off for a massage. Fortunately I have a Heartfelt Tributes programme on my computer. All I have to do, in theory, is tap in the recipient's name – John Cleese, The Queen Mother, Saddam Hussein – and Hey presto! Microsoft does the business, and I'm on the table beneath Suki's healing, if not yet fully licensed hands, within the hour. So, here goes, install programme and press 'Enter'.

A Heartfelt Tribute to John Cleese

John Cleese is one of those rare people, like Bill Gates, who has been blessed with enormous natural talent and, more importantly, the ability to harness it for the good of mankind. In the same way that Bill Gates was able to realise his vision of, quite literally creating a new world order through his own single-minded brilliance in the creation of computer technology, so John Cleese has done whatever he has done so well.

Bill Gates, unlike the Queen Mother, is not a man who flaunts his own personal power. He is essentially a modest man. A man whose only hope is that the world becomes a better place to live in, that it becomes a world where, thanks to spell-check and effective file management, little children cease to cry and animals give milk and the halt walk and the lame dance and people with no talent for anything just buy the stuff and shut up and let people like John and Bill and Saddam get on with what they do best...
RUNNING THE WORLD !!!!!!!

Some kind of virus seems to have crept into the Heartfelt Tributes '97 programme, either that or I'm not using it properly, so I shall have to do the damn preface myself and put Suki off until tomorrow and hope that the groin strain doesn't get any worse. Sorry about all this. I'll be as quick as I can.

John Cleese - The Writer's writer.
A personal appreciation by Michael Palin.

John loves words, particularly 'nebulous', 'trenchant' and 'orthodontic'. Though most children's first word is 'mama', John's was 'elision'. 'Mama' was third, after 'hydraulics'.

Even his birthplace, Weston-Super-Mare, had two words more than most people's birthplaces. He has written many words for Monty Python, some of which like 'parrot', 'cheese' and 'breasts' have gone down in history.

Rumours abound about this tower of talent, ranging from the fantastic - he once tunnelled under the Grand National course at Aintree and stuck a spoon up through the turf five days after the race had passed - through the frankly unlikely - he can take out his intestines and put them back again without surgery, to the intriguing - he is related on his mother's side to Prester John. Whatever the truth about this deeply private man one thing is certain, he was born with a silver tongue in his mouth.

John's favourite authors are eighteen and female.

M.P. June 1999

Eric the half a bee

Half a bee, philosophically,
Must, ipso facto, half not be.
But half the bee has got to be,
Vis-à-vis its entity. D'you see?
But can a bee be said to be,
Or not to be, an entire bee,
When half the bee is not a bee,
Due to some ancient injury?

La di di, one two three,
Eric the half a bee.
A b c d e f g,
Eric the half a bee.

Is this wretched demi-bee,
Half asleep upon my knee,
Some freak from a menagerie?
No! It's Eric the half a bee.

Fiddle di dum, fiddle di dee,
Eric the half a bee.
Ho ho ho,
Tee hee hee,
Eric the half a bee.

I love this hive employ ee ee,
Bisected accidentally,
One summer afternoon by me,
I love him carnally.
Semi-carnally.
The end.

Cyril Connolly?

No, semi-carnally!

Oh.

ANNE ELK'S
THEORY

PRESENTER: I have with me tonight an elk. Oh! *Anne* Elk.

MISS ELK: Miss Anne Elk

PRESENTER: Now I understand you have a new theory about the brontosaurus, Miss Elk.

MISS ELK: Can I just say here Chris, for one moment, that I have a new theory about the brontosaurus?

PRESENTER: Exactly ... What is it?

MISS ELK: Where?

PRESENTER: No, no, your new theory.

MISS ELK: Oh! What is my theory?

PRESENTER: Yes.

MISS ELK: Oh what is my theory, that it is. Well Chris, you may well ask me what is my theory.

PRESENTER: ... Yes, I *am* asking you.

MISS ELK: Thank you, Chris. Well Chris, what is it, that it is - this theory of mine? Well, this is what it is - my theory that I have, that is to say, which is mine ... is mine.

PRESENTER: ... Yes, I *know* it's yours, but what is it?

MISS ELK: Where? Oh, what is my theory? This is it. *(She clears her throat at some length)* My theory, that belongs to me, is as follows. *(She clears her throat at greater length)* This is how it goes. The next thing that I am going to say, is my theory. Ready?

PRESENTER: Yes!

MISS ELK: My theory by A. Elk. Brackets, Miss, brackets. This theory goes as follows, and begins now. All brontosauruses are thin at one end, much much thicker in the middle and then thin again at the far end. That is my theory, which is mine, and belongs to me and I own it, and what it is too.

thinner

thicker

thinner

PRESENTER: ... That's it, is it?

MISS ELK: Spot on, Chris.

PRESENTER: Well, this theory of yours appears to have ... er ... hit the nail on the head.

MISS ELK: *And* it's mine.

PRESENTER: Yes, well thank you very much for coming along to the studio.

MISS ELK: My pleasure, Chris.

The National Institute of Historical Research (*Founded 1973*) Proudly Announce

The Official Medallic Commemoration of the History of Mankind

Hallmarked First Edition Proof Sets in solid Welsh Silver* are available ONLY by advance covenanted subscription or, of course, cash. To preserve value, the number of sets minted must be strictly limited to the number we can actually sell. No more will be minted after this number is reached, in order to guarantee rarity.

This Magnificent Set of Shiny Bright Objects will be of particular interest, not only to everyone, but especially to Collectors of Objets d'Art and Jackdaws.

ABSOLUTELY FREE!

All Hallmarked First Edition Proof Sets are clearly marked 'Hallmarked First Edition Proof Set' to distinguish them from Non-Hallmarked First Edition Proof Sets, and Hallmarked Second (or Third) Edition Proof Sets, and Hallmarked First Edition Non-Proof Sets, none of which exists. However the words 'Hallmarked First Edition' and 'Proof' have associations with objects of value and so are clearly marked on these medallions.

**A very attractive and valuable Zinc / Bakelite alloy*

*Jack Hobbs stabbed in his
bath by Charlotte Rampling*

*Napoleon forging luncheon
vouchers*

*Marie Curie eludes Nero's
troops by hiding in a lift*

*Leonardo da Vinci nearly
inventing Canasta*

*George Washington shortly
before intercourse with Mary
Baker Eddy*

Oliver Cromwell in Stand
by Your Bedouin *with
Brian Rix*

*Peter the Great carving his
initials on a passing vicar*

*Mrs René Descartes
sleeping*

The vital, dramatic and very fascinating history of Man himself, which will be of
particular interest to all human beings, is now to be made official, by the issue of these
fine medallions, with nice pictures on them, and not too many words.

RAYMOND
LUXURY YACHT

INTERVIEWER: Good evening. I have with me in the studio tonight one of Britain's leading skin specialists – Raymond Luxury Yacht.

RAYMOND: That's not my name.

INTERVIEWER: I'm sorry.

RAYMOND: It's spelt Raymond Luxury Yacht, but it's pronounced 'Throatwobbler Mangrove'.

INTERVIEWER: ...You're a very silly man and I'm not going to interview you.

RAYMOND: Ah, anti-Semitism!

INTERVIEWER: ...Not at all. That's not even a proper nose. It's polystyrene.

He takes Raymond's nose off.

RAYMOND: Give me my nose back.

INTERVIEWER: You can collect it at reception. Now go away.

RAYMOND: I want to be on the television.

INTERVIEWER: Well you can't.

African Notebook

by Col. B. B. Wakenham-Palsh M.C., O.B.E.

Chapter 19
A Lucky Escape

The next day I decided to take my usual pre-breakfast 'stroll', as I used to call it, into the *majambi,* or jungle, to see if I could catch sight of the very rare 'Chukawati Bati' or Bird of Purgatory, which 'Trusty' as we all called our faithful native *ghabi* or guide had reported seeing the previous *latbani* (evening) while we were looking for Harry's leg.

I had only been 'strolling' along the *majambi* (jungle) *ortobam* (path) for a few minutes when I became aware of a large and rather fierce *fritbangowonkabwaki,* or lion, which was standing partially hidden in the *pteee,* or clearing. I had strayed so close to him, absorbed as I was in my ornithological *questi* (quest) that when the splendid old thing opened its massive *goti* (jaws) to roar, revealing as fine a *womba,* or set, of teeth as I have seen in an adult male, I could, without so much as leaning forward, have taken his magnificent uvula in my left hand. Taking advantage of my good luck, I did so, tweaking it hard, an old English colonial officer's *granwi,* or trick. This bemused the lion and so I was able to get in a couple of good straight lefts, keeping my guard up well, to his upper palate and follow them with a cracking good right cross, moving my weight into the punch (as old 'Buffy' Spalding had taught me so many years ago, prior to the needle

11

match against Uppington when 'Spindly' Crabber got up off the floor six times so pluckily only just to fail to win the draw which would have halved the *batwel* or match), right into my opponent's mane. Then dancing back a couple of paces, I weaved about causing *fritbangowonkabwaki* to miss wildly with his crude haymakers while I notched up a few useful points with my left *swati,* or hand, and I soon found that by this simple strategy of keeping him from getting in close, where his mighty jaws could have done a lot of *nagasaki,* or damage, I could pick him off pretty much at leisure. In fact it was only after some *twenti (*twenty) minutes that I happened to glance around the clearing to discover that our contest was now being watched by a circle of some fifteen odd of *fritbangowonkabwaki's* chums, some of whom were already beginning to edge forward, manes bristling and teeth akimbo, towards our good selves.

It was the work of a moment to divine from their magnificent expressions that they were taking a decidedly partisan attitude to our match, and that they would have few qualms about joining in on my opponent's side if necessary; and so, judging that, if they did, they would eventually subdue me by sheer weight of numbers, I took the better part of valour, and feinting away from another of *fritbangowonkabwaki's* wild rushes, I got in a parting short jab to the

 base of his tail (not a blow I was proud of, although it put him down for several minutes, but which I felt was excused by the exigencies of the situation, due, after all, to the unsporting behaviour of his colleagues in the first place) before springing upwards towards a lowly hanging branch of an enormous *bwinda tree* (a species related distantly to our own *Elm* (elm), but easily distinguishable

by its broad unevenly veined leaf, with its characteristic cheetah's paw shape, and the peculiar purple-ochre colour of the outer leaves of its *gimbi*, or buds), some fifteen feet

above my head. I had leapt not a moment too soon, for, although I had gained a firm grasp upon the handy branch, two of *fritbangowonkabwaki's* pals, leaping with me, had each seized one of my trusty boots in their jaws whilst a third had succeeded in firmly embedding his *fangi* (teeth) in the seat of my pants, albeit not in my *sit-upon* itself, but in the surrounding material thereof. What a strange sight I must have made, hanging unshaven from the branch with three enormous lions attached to me! It was not, indeed, without difficulty that I pulled myself up until I could take the branch in my mouth, thus freeing my hands for the more important work of detaching the determined trio, whose bites, however, proved to be so *woki*, or vice-like, that I eventually decided, not without regret, that it was only by actually abandoning the relevant apparel that I could free myself of their attentions.

Unlacing a jungle boot while hanging by one's teeth from a tree with three angry lions attached is not as easy as it might seem, especially when the lions concerned are being urged on to even greater efforts by the highly vocal support of their companions beneath, but eventually it was done, and right boot and lion plummeted back into the clearing, followed rapidly by their opposite numbers. With the vastly reduced load the shorts were a formality and in a trice I was seated comfortably on the branch looking down at the enraged pride beneath, who by now, incidentally, must have numbered well over a hundred. However, by now I was feeling distinctly peckish , and so doffing my *sola topi* rather humorously in their direction I turned for home and breakfast.

As I made my way back to camp through the trees some *jambotwanibokotwikatwanafryingpanibwanabotomafekazami* (five) minutes later, with the lions still pursuing me below, I saw that I had reached the Wananga River. To my delight, I spotted a solitary creeper suspended from a tree just upstream, across the cascading torrent, to the forest the other side. Ideal! Soon I was well on my way towards the far bank, admiring the magnificent view of the

 raging Wananga directly beneath. However, I was still not half-way across when I began to realise that my 'creeper' was not all it might be, and looking towards the far end of it I was astonished to see, staring back at me from a wak-wak tree, the unmistakable square head, yellow-green criss-cross markings and fearful fangs of an anaconda! I will admit I was astounded! An anaconda in Africa! And what is more, one that clearly took exception to being demoted to viaduct. With one mighty flick of its rippling body, I was sent spinning high, high up into the air, where I had to dodge a passing eagle, before being able to plunge downwards into the waiting *ouse* (river).

I had already surmised that my new surroundings would pose a different problem, for the Wananga is notorious for both the quantity of its hippopotamus and crocodile, and also for the degree of rancour with which these two species regard the human race, and sure enough, on surfacing, I saw the huge shapes of the former setting off towards me from their station upstream, while several thousand of the latter bore down on me from the other direction; so, making the best of a bad job, I swam straight at the nearest crocodile, waited until he opened his enormous jaws and then quick as a flash spurted forward and, snatching a full lungful of air, hurled myself into his mouth, pulling the jaws shut after me, and scrambled down his throat, while he was still surprised, to the relative safety of his stomach, where I stayed, holding my breath, until I guessed the coast was clear. Then gambling all on a quick getaway, I worked my way back up his thorax and started insistently tickling the back of his throat. I did not have long to wait, for the jaws opened suddenly and I was hurled out into the light of day by the force of the mightiest cough I have ever experienced at such close quarters, right onto the bank of the river, believe it or not about ten yards from the point where the rest of the fellows were just tucking into their devilled kidneys. I must say they were pretty amused to see me appearing from a nearby crocodile without my shorts, but I took their jesting in good part and had soon rejoined them to salvage what I could from the pan of kidneys.

It may seem that I have rather padded out a commonplace enough tale, but the real reason that I have recounted my adventure in perhaps rather unnecessary detail is that *exactly* the same thing happened to my wife the very next day.

CONSULTING JEAN-PAUL SARTRE

MRS CONCLUSION: Hello, Mrs Premise.

MRS PREMISE: Hello, Mrs Conclusion.

MRS CONCLUSION: Busy day?

MRS PREMISE: Busy! I've just spent four hours burying the cat.

MRS CONCLUSION: *Four* hours to bury a cat?

MRS PREMISE: Yes! It wouldn't keep still, wriggling about, howling its head off.

MRS CONCLUSION: Oh – it wasn't dead then?

MRS PREMISE: Well, no, no, but it's not at all a well cat, so as we were going away for a fortnight's holiday, I thought I'd better bury it, just to be on the safe side.

MRS CONCLUSION: Quite right. You don't want to come back from Sorrento to a dead cat. That's bathos that is. Yes, kill it now, that's what I say. We're going to have our budgie put down.

MRS PREMISE: Is it very old?

MRS CONCLUSION: No, we just don't like it. We're going to take it to the vet tomorrow.

16

MRS PREMISE: Tell me, how do they put budgies down then?

MRS CONCLUSION: Well it's funny you should ask that, but I've just been reading a great big book about how to put your budgie down, and apparently you can either hit them with the book, or, you can shoot them just there, just above the beak.

MRS PREMISE: Well well well. 'Course, Mrs Essence flushed hers down the loo.

MRS CONCLUSION: Ooh! No! You shouldn't do that   it's dangerous. They breed in the sewers, and eventually you get evil-smelling flocks of huge soiled budgies flying out of people's lavatories infringing their personal freedom.

MRS PREMISE: It's a funny thing freedom. I mean how can any of us be really free when we still have personal possessions?

MRS CONCLUSION: You can't. I mean, how can I go off and join Frelimo when I've got nine more instalments to pay on the fridge?

MRS PREMISE: Well this is the whole crux of Jean-Paul Sartre's *Roads to Freedom*.

MRS CONCLUSION: No, it bloody isn't. The nub of that is, his characters stand for all of us in their desire to avoid action. Mind you, the man at the off-licence says it's an everyday story of French country folk.

MRS PREMISE: What does he know? Sixty new pence for a bottle of Maltese Claret! Well I personally think Jean-Paul's masterwork is an allegory of man's search for commitment.

MRS CONCLUSION: No it isn't.

MRS PREMISE: All right. We can soon settle this. We'll ask him.

MRS CONCLUSION: ... Do you know him?

MRS PREMISE: Yes, we met on holiday last year.

MRS CONCLUSION: In Ibiza!?

MRS PREMISE: Off we go.

MRS PREMISE: Oh look, Paris!

Mrs Conclusion and Mrs Premise walk up to the front door of an apartment block. On the front door is a list of the inhabitants of the block.

4. JEAN GENET & FRIEND

8. *Mr René Descartes (junior)*

FLAT 3 JACQUES COUSTEAU

7. Jean-Paul Sartre et Betty-Muriel Sartre

2 *Yves Montand*

flat 6 Indira Gandhi

Flat 1 Duke & Duchess of Windsor

FLAT 5. MARCEL MARCEAU WALKING AGAINST THE WIND LIMITED

MRS SARTRE: Hello, love!

MRS PREMISE: Hello! Oh this is Mrs Conclusion from No.46.

MRS SARTRE: Nice to meet you, dear.

MRS CONCLUSION: Bonjour.

MRS PREMISE: How's the old man, then?

MRS SARTRE: Oh, don't ask. He's in one of his bleeding moods. 'The bourgeoisie *this*, the bourgeoisie *that*'...

MRS PREMISE: Can we have a word with him?

MRS SARTRE: Yes.

MRS CONCLUSION: Thank you.

Mrs Premise and Mrs Conclusion go and knock on the door of Jean-Paul's room.

MRS PREMISE: Coo-ee! Jean-Paul?

JEAN-PAUL'S VOICE: Oui?

MRS PREMISE: Jean-Paul. Your famous trilogy *Les Chemins de la Liberté*, is it an allegory of man's search for commitment?

JEAN-PAUL'S VOICE: Oui.

MRS PREMISE: I told you so!

MRS CONCLUSION: Oh *sugar*!

WE'RE ALL INDIVIDUALS

BRIAN wakes, stretches and goes to
open his bedroom shutters.

CROWD: HOSANNA!!

BRIAN: ...good morning.

CROWD: A blessing! A blessing!

BRIAN: No, please. Please!! Please listen...

The crowd quietens.

BRIAN: I've got one or two things to say.

CROWD: Tell us. Tell us *both* of them!!

BRIAN: Look ... you've got it all wrong. You don't need to follow me. You don't need to follow anybody. You've got to think for yourselves — you're all individuals.

CROWD: Yes, we're all individuals.

BRIAN: You are all *different*.

CROWD: Yes, we are all different.

MAN: I'm not.

CROWD: ssshhh!

BRIAN: ...well, that's it. You've all got to work it out for *yourselves*...

CROWD: Yes, yes!! We've got to work it out for *ourselves*...

BRIAN: Exactly.

CROWD: ....Tell us *more*!!!!

THE PYTHON PANEL

Ruth Frampton: Britain's first woman judge and a leading exponent of Women's Lib.
Vice-Pope Eric: the No. 2 man in the Vatican.
Brian Stalin: eldest brother of the USSR's late great Dictator.
Dr Edward Kraszt: American sociologist and author of All Anyone Need Know About Anything.

PYTHON: Good evening.

ALL EXCEPT KRASZT: Good evening.

KRASZT: I didn't say 'Good evening' then because I wanted a line to myself.

PYTHON: We take your point, Dr Kraszt. Vice-Pope Eric?

VICE-POPE: Not at the moment, thank you.

PYTHON: Brian?

STALIN: I'm fine thanks. How about Miss Frampton?

PYTHON: Well we are going to ask her our first question so that's not really necessary.

ALL: Fine.

PYTHON: Ruth Frampton, in 1959 you became the first woman to become a judge of Quarter Sessions in this country.

FRAMPTON: My first line is just to say 'That's right'.

PYTHON: Why do you claim to be Sir Edmund Hillary's mother?

STALIN: What? I've never said I ...

PYTHON: No, we were talking to Miss Frampton.

STALIN: Sorry, I thought you were looking at me.

KRASZT: It's a bit confusing you know.

PYTHON: Shut up please. (*Laughter*)

KRASZT: I didn't hear anyone laugh.

PYTHON: To return to our question. Why do you claim a maternal situation vis-à-vis the first conqueror of Everest?

FRAMPTON Because I *am* his mum. He is my little Edmund, bless his little pitons, and he has been a wonderful boy to me.

PYTHON: But Sir Edmund has it on record that he knows his mother well and that she and you are definitely separate persons.

FRAMPTON: Then he is being naughty because he is over-tired. All boys are naughty sometimes; to expect them to be perfect is quintessentially daft.

PYTHON: Dr. Kraszt?

KRASZT: This is probably correct. The recent survey of 420,000 people, carried out at Michigan University over a period of eight years by Professors Rinehart, Schwartz, Zincotcin and Semite, indicates conclusively that people – not just boys, interestingly enough – are by and large not absolutely perfect. A statistically significant proportion of them, at some stage in the 70-odd-years maturation process, do something that they ought not to really. These findings constitute something of a breakthrough in this field.

PYTHON: Thank you Dr. Kraszt.

FRAMPTON: You see? So I am *definitely* his mother.

PYTHON: But were you actually present at his birth?

FRAMPTON: No. I can't claim that. At the time I was unavoidably detained at the Hague, where I had the honour to represent my country in the International Legal Championships. Edmund knows it was impossible for me to be there and has never held it against me.

STALIN: Then why is he applying for an injunction against the publication of your forthcoming book?

FRAMPTON: Because, Brian, I reveal in *My Son, The Clambering Knight* that before the final assault, he tied a large weight to Tensing so that he could get to the top first.

STALIN: Tensing's mother has confirmed this story to me. The weight, incidentally, is now in the Tensing Family Museum on K2 along with other Sherpa-connected objects.

FRAMPTON: Anyway Eddie is excrementally scared that when this gets out they will confiscate his knighthood, which would cost him a few bob in directorships. Even so, I think he has overreacted.

KRASZT: This can happen of course. People do sometimes overreact to things – that is to say, when things happen, these people – in fact, all of us occasionally react over-wise, as it were, to these very things. To put it another way, a perfectly ordinary stimulus produces an overreaction, O. This has been shown time and time again by studies undertaken by the Californian Institute for Making Studies under Luxurious Conditions.

FRAMPTON: Exactly. Anyway, Eddie is a Kiwi poppet; it is this woman who happened to be around when he came to light who is playing dog in the manger.

PYTHON: To change the subject, how

about sex?

FRAMPTON: Sex is a fine and wonderful gift provided that it is accompanied by a feeling of love and involvement for whoever it is you happen to be banging away with at the time.

PENTHOUSE: How about pubic hair?

PYTHON: Come out from behind those curtains! Now go away and take your ludicrous catchphrases with you.

PENTHOUSE: Sorry. *(exeunt)*

PYTHON: So a feeling of love and involvement is necessary?

FRAMPTON: Or at least a reasonable pretence of it.

KRASZT: I think it's important to distinguish between premarital sex, that is sex before marriage, extra-marital sex, that is sex outside a marriage, or extra sex within; pseudo-marital sex, which is marital sex where the marriage is invalid due to an oversight in the ceremony or mistaken identity; ultra-marital sex, which is sex over and above the marital sex, quasi-marital sex where the two partners, being married, believe themselves to be making love when in fact they are not; post-marital sex which is sex after the marriage or after the divorce; and amarital sex, which is sheer simple-minded, out-of-context banging. Then there is pre-sexual marriage where the spouses are unusually timid, busy or

maladroit; extra-sexual marriage wh...

PYTHON: Vice-Pope Eric? What is the Catholic position?

VICE-POPE: Well our main worry at this stage is intra-marital sex.

PYTHON: Sex *within* the marriage.

KRASZT: I missed that.

VICE-POPE: You see, it's *within* marriage, people tend to forget, that most of this carnal knowing takes place.

PYTHON: But *that* isn't wrong from a Catholic point of view?

VICE-POPE: Well, actually ... it is. Yes. I mean we don't often come straight out with it because our problem is that ... like it or not, sex, at this moment in time, is still the best method we've got of reproducing ourselves. I mean we certainly recommend virgin births where possible, but we can't rely on them, so for purely practical reasons we've been forced to turn a blind eye to intra-marital sex *for the time being*. But only, of course, for outnumbering purposes; not for *fun*.

KRASZT: Which is why you will not allow any form of contraception.

VICE-POPE: Exactly.

FRAMPTON: But you allow the rhythm method!

VICE-POPE: Ah, but only because it doesn't work.

PYTHON: But are you not worried that the population explosion may lead to

greater poverty, disease and eventually war?

VICE-POPE: Well, you must remember, our concern is for the next world. So the quicker we can get people there the better.

FRAMPTON: Your vice-holiness, can you advise me how I should tell Eddie about sex. Whenever I try to bring the subject up casually, he becomes embarrassed.

VICE-POPE: Well, frankly, it's not easy. I mean, take the sex act. Please. *(Laughter)* Well, none of us can work out what God must have been thinking of when He dreamed it up. I mean...you know what people actually do, do you? It's a mind boggler isn't it! Going to the lavatory is bad enough, but

PYTHON: Vice-Pope, did Christ himself say anything about sex being sinful?

VICE-POPE: Apparently not, no. This was obviously an oversight on his part, which fortunately we have been able to rectify, with the help of the teachings of Paul ...

PYTHON: Oh, the pouf.

FRAMPTON: Does this necessity to sub-edit Christ sometimes worry you?

VICE-POPE: Not really. After all, you can't treat the New Testament as gospel. And one must remember that Christ, though he was a fine young man with some damn good ideas, did go off the rails now and again, rich-man-eye-of-

camel, for example.

KRASZT: But with certain exceptions, you accept his teaching?

VICE-POPE: Oh yes, it's been an invaluable basis for our whole operation really. Of course people accuse us of not practising what we preach, but you must remember that if you're trying to propagate a creed of poverty, gentleness and tolerance, you need a very rich, powerful organisation to do it.

FRAMPTON: I'm afraid I must go now. I have to get Eddie's tea ready.

PYTHON: Well, we've almost finished.

STALIN: But I want to tell you about being Joe Stalin's elder brother. What it felt like to grow up in a family where a tiny child was organising purges all the time! The knock at the nursery door in the middle of the night, the way Joe got rid of Dad and had Auntie Vanya installed as a puppet-father, how he got our smallest sister, Catherina, made eldest brother by giving the dog a vote! How can I tell all that in seven lines?

PYTHON: Six.

STALIN: Well I soon realised the way things were going after all the shooting at Boris's Christening, so I packed my worldly goods and with jaunty step set off for the legendary city of Dundee, in Scotland.

PYTHON: Sorry. That's it.

STALIN: Can't I go on down here?
PYTHON: No. It doesn't look nice.

LARCH
IN COURT

JUDGE: Mr Larch, is there anything you wish to say before I pass sentence?

PRISONER: Well ... I'd just like to say, m'lud, I've got a family ... a wife and six kids ... and I hope very much you don't have to take away my freedom ... because ... well, freedom is a state much prized within the realm of civilised society. It is a bond wherewith the savage man may charm the outward hatchments of his soul, and soothe the troubled breast into a magnitude of quiet. It is most precious as a blessed balm, the saviour of princes, the harbinger of happiness, yea, the very stuff and pith of all we hold most dear. What frees the prisoner in his lonely cell, chained within the bondage of rude walls, far the from the owl of Thebes? What fires and stirs the woodcock in his springe or wakes the drowsy apricot betides? What goddess doth the storm toss'd mariner offer her most tempestuous prayers to? Freedom! Freedom!! Freedom!!!

JUDGE: It's only a bloody parking offence.

COUNSEL: I'm sorry I'm late m'lud, I couldn't find a kosher car park. Please don't bother to recap, I'll pick it up as we go along. Call Mrs Fiona Lewis.

CLERK OF THE COURT: Call Mrs Fiona Lewis!

MRS LEWIS: I swear to tell the truth, the whole truth and nothing but the truth, so *anyway*, I said to her, I said, they can't afford that on what he earns, I mean for a start the feathers get up your nose, I ask you, four and six a pound, and him with a wooden leg, I don't know how she puts up with it after all the trouble she's had with her you-know-what, anyway it was a white wedding much to everyone's surprise, of course they bought everything on the hire purchase, I think they ought to send them back where they came from, I mean you've got to be cruel to be kind so Mrs Harris said, so she said, she said, dead crab she said, she said!

27

Well, her sister's gone to Rhodesia what with her womb and all, and her youngest, her youngest as thin as a filing cabinet, and the goldfish, the goldfish they've got whooping cough they keep spitting water all over their Bratbys, well they do don't they, I mean you *can't* can you, I mean they're not even married or anything, they're not even *divorced*, and he's in the KGB if you ask me, he says that he's a tree surgeon but I don't like the sound of his liver, all that squeaking and banging every night till the small hours, his mother's been much better since she had her head off, yes she has, I said, don't you talk to me about bladders, I said...

MRS LEWIS is carried out of court still talking.

JUDGE: Mr Bartlett, I fail to see the relevance of your last witness.

COUNSEL: My next witness will explain that if m'ludship will allow. Call the late Arthur Aldridge.

JUDGE: The *late* Arthur Aldridge?

JUDGE: Is your witness dead?

COUNSEL: Well ... virtually, m'lud.

JUDGE: He's not completely dead?

COUNSEL: No he's not completely dead m'lud. But he's not at all well.

JUDGE: But if he's not dead, what's he doing in a coffin?

COUNSEL: Oh, it's purely a precaution m'lud – if I may continue? Mr Aldridge, you were a ... you *are* a stockbroker of 10 Savundra Close, Wimbledon.

There is a sound of a knock from the coffin

JUDGE: What was that knock?

COUNSEL: It means 'yes' m'lud. One knock for 'yes', and two knocks for 'no'. Mr Aldridge, would it be fair to say that you are not at all well?

Another knock is heard

In fact Mr Aldridge, not to put too fine a point on it, would you be prepared to say that you are, as it were, what is generally known as, in a manner of speaking, 'dead'? Mr Aldridge I put it to you that you are dead.

COUNSEL: No further questions m'lud.

JUDGE: What do you mean, no further questions? You can't just dump a dead body in my court and say 'no further questions'. I demand an explanation.

COUNSEL: There are no easy answers in this case m'lud.

JUDGE: You haven't the slightest idea what this case is about.

COUNSEL: M'lud, the strange, damnable, almost diabolic threads of this extraordinary tangled web of intrigue will shortly, m'lud, reveal a plot so fiendish, so infernal, so heinous...

JUDGE: Mr Bartlett, your client has already pleaded guilty to the parking offence.

COUNSEL: Parking offence, schmarking offence, m'lud. We must leave no stone unturned. Call Cardinal Richelieu.

JUDGE: Cardinal Richelieu?!?!

CARDINAL: 'Allo everyone, it's wonderful to be 'ere y'know, I just love your country. London is so beautiful at this time of year.

COUNSEL: You are Cardinal Armand du Plessis de Richelieu, First Minister of Louis XIII?

CARDINAL: Oui.

COUNSEL: Cardinal, would it be fair to say that you not only built up the centralized monarchy in France but also perpetuated the religious schism in Europe?

CARDINAL: That's what they say.

COUNSEL: Did you persecute the Huguenots and take even sterner measures against the great Catholic nobles who made common cause with foreign foes in defence of their feudal independence?

CARDINAL: I sure did that thing.

COUNSEL: Speaking as a Cardinal of the Roman Catholic Church, as

First Minister of Louis XIII, and as one of the architects of the modern world already – would you say that Harold Larch was a man of good character?

CARDINAL: Listen! Harry is a very wonderful human being.

Enter INSPECTOR DIM.

DIM: Not so fast!

PRISONER: Why not?

DIM: Well, I'm Dim.

ALL: Dim of the Yard!!

DIM: Yes, and I've a few questions I'd like to ask Cardinal so-called Richelieu.

CARDINAL: Bonjour, Monsieur Dim.

DIM: So-called Cardinal, I put it to you that you died in December 1642.

CARDINAL: That is correct.

DIM: Ah ha! He fell for my little trap.

The court applauds and the CARDINAL *looks dismayed.*

COUNSEL: My life you're clever, Dim. He'd certainly taken me in.

DIM: It's all in a day's work.

JUDGE: With a brilliant mind like yours, Dim, you could be something other than a policeman.

DIM: Yes.

JUDGE: What?

DIM *(singing)*: If I were not in the CID
Something else I'd like to be
If I were not in the CID
A window cleaner, me!

JUDGE: Silence! The fine is thirty shillings. Court adjourned.

FEAR NO MAN!

ABSOLUTELY FREE!

I'll make you a MASTER of LLAP-Goch

...the Secret Welsh ART of SELF DEFENCE that requires NO INTELLIGENCE, STRENGTH or PHYSICAL COURAGE.

The FANTASTIC SECRETS of the SECRET world-famous method of SELF-DEFENCE, kept secret for centuries because of their DEADLY POWER to MAIM, KILL, SMASH, BATTER, FRACTURE, CRUSH, DISMEMBER, CRACK, DISEMBOWEL, CRIPPLE, SNAP are now revealed to YOU in the English Language by a LLAP-GOCH master AT HIS OWN RISK, PROVIDED you promise to MAIM, CRUSH, DISEMBOWEL and so on ONLY in SELF DEFENCE.* *This is just to cover ourselves, as you will understand.

WHO IS THIS MAN? This is the LLAP-GOCH MASTER who will reveal to YOU the SECRETS of LAPP. GOCH HE IS A FULLY QUALIFIED leek-coloured BELT FIRST DAI MASTER and cares nothing for the penal reform.

WHY "At his own risk"?

BECAUSE if his fellow masters of LLAP-GOCH DISCOVER his IDENTITY, they will PUNISH HIM SEVERELY for revealing the DEADLY secrets he had promised to keep SECRET, without giving them a piece of the ACTION, and also BECAUSE of the TERRIBLE risk of PUNISHMENT he runs under the Trades Description Act.

WHAT is LLAP-GOCH?

IT is THE most DEADLY form of SECRET self-DEFENCE that HAS ever been widely advertised and available to EVERYONE.

WHY ALL the CAPITALS?

Because THE most likely kind of person TO answer THIS kind of advertisement HAS less trouble under-STANDING words if they ARE written in BIG letters.

WHAT is LLAP-GOCH again?

It is an ANCIENT Welsh ART based on a BRILLIANTLY simple I-D-E-A, that the most VITAL element of ATTACK is SURPRISE Therefore ... the BEST way to protect yourself AGAINST any ASSAILANT is to ATTACK him before he attacks YOU... Or BETTER ... BEFORE the THOUGHT of doing so has EVEN OCCURRED TO HIM!!!

SO YOU MAY BE ABLE TO RENDER YOUR ASSAILENT *UNCONSCIOUS* BEFORE He is even aware of your very existance!

BANISH INADEQUACY

No longer need you feel WEAK, helpless, INDECISIVE, NOT fascinating and ASHAMED of your genital dimentions. No more need you be out-manoeuvred in political debate!! GOOD BYE HUMILIATION, Wisecracking bullies, Karate experts, boxing champions, sarcastic vicars, traffic wardens, entire panzer divisions will melt to pulp as you master every situation without INADEQUACY. PROTECT YOUR LOVED ONES. You will no longer look pitiful and spotty to your GIRL FRIENDS when you leave some unsuspecting passer-by 'looking like four tins of cat food'. They will admire you for your MASTERY and DECISIVENESS and LACK OF you for your MASTERY and DECISIVENESS and LACK OF INADEQUACY and will almost certainly let you put your HAND inside their BLOUSE out of sheer ADMIRATION and after seeing more of your expert disabling they'll almost definitely go to bed with you .

Why WELSH Art?

Llap-Goch was developed in Wales because for the average Welshman, the best prospects of achieving a reasonable standard of living lie with the aquisition of the most efficient techniques of armed robbery.

How do I learn?

No, you mean 'How do *you* learn'. I know already

How do you learn?

You receive ABSOLUTELY FREE your own special personal LLAP-GOCH Picture Book with hundreds of PHOTOGRAPHS and just very few plain, clear and simple, easy to understand words.

Only a FOUR-SECOND WORK-OUT Each Day!

and you will be ready to HARM people, DEVELOP UP TO 38" BICEPS, GROW UP TO 12" TALLER, LOSE UP TO 40" OF FAT IN YOUR FIRST WORK-OUT! PROLONG YOUR LIFE BY *UP TO* 1,000 YEARS. GO TO BED WITH UP TO ANY LUDICROUS NUMBER OF GIRLS YOU CARE TO THINK OF PROVIDING YOU REALISE THIS STATEMENT IS QUITE MEANINGLESS AS THE PHRASE UP TO CLEARLY INCLUDES THE NUMBER 'NOUGHT'.

What Does it Cost?

This, like LLAP-GOCH, is a SECRET but you will find out sooner or later, don't worry.

THE MERCHANT BANKER

COLLECTOR: Thank you for seeing me. My name is Phillips.

BANKER: How do you do. I'm a merchant banker.

COLLECTOR: How do you do Mr...

BANKER: Er ... I forget my name for the moment, but I am a merchant banker.

COLLECTOR: I wondered whether you'd like to contribute to the orphans' home.

BANKER: Well actually here at Slater Nazi we are quite keen to get into orphans, you know, developing market and all that ... what sort of sum did you have in mind?

COLLECTOR: Well ... er ... you're a rich man.

BANKER: Yes, I am. Yes. Yes, very very rich. Quite phenomenally wealthy. I do own the most startling quantities of cash. Yes, quite right ... you're a smart young lad aren't you?

COLLECTOR: Thank you, sir.

BANKER: Now, as you were saying, I'm very, very, very, very, very, very, very, very, very, very rich.

COLLECTOR: So er, how about a pound?

BANKER: A pound. Yes, I see. Now this loan would be secured by the ...

COLLECTOR: It's not a loan, sir.

BANKER : What?

COLLECTOR: It's not a loan.

BANKER: Ah.

COLLECTOR: You get one of these little flags, sir.

BANKER: It's a bit small for a share certificate isn't it? Look, I think I'd better run this over to our legal department. If you could possibly pop back on Friday

COLLECTOR: Well do you have to do that, couldn't you just give me the pound?

BANKER: Yes, but you see I don't know what it's *for*.

COLLECTOR: It's for the orphans.

BANKER: ...Yes.

COLLECTOR: It's a gift.

BANKER: A what?

COLLECTOR: A gift.

BANKER: Oh a *gift!* A tax dodge.

COLLECTOR: No, no, no, no.

BANKER: No? Well, I'm awfully sorry I don't understand. Can you just explain exactly what you want?

COLLECTOR: Well, I want you to give me a pound, and then I go away and give it to the orphans.

BANKER: Go on.

COLLECTOR: Well, that's it.

BANKER: ...No, no, no, I don't follow this at all, I mean, I don't want to seem stupid but it looks to me as though I'm a pound down on the whole deal.

COLLECTOR: Well, yes you are.

BANKER: I *am!* Well, what is my incentive to give you the pound?

COLLECTOR: Well the incentive is – to make the orphans happy.

BANKER: Are you quite sure you've got this right?

COLLECTOR: Yes, *lots* of people give me money.

BANKER: What, just like that?

COLLECTOR: Yes.

BANKER: Must be sick. I don't suppose you could give me a list of their names and addresses could you?

COLLECTOR: No, I just go up to them in the street and ask.

BANKER: Good lord! That's the most exciting new idea I've heard in years! It's so simple it's brilliant! Well, if that idea of yours isn't worth a pound I'd like to know what is.

COLLECTOR: Oh, thank you sir.

BANKER: The only trouble is, you gave me the idea before I'd given you the pound. And that's not good business.

COLLECTOR: Isn't it?

BANKER: No I'm afraid it isn't. So, off you go!

He presses a button

BANKER: Nice to do business with you.

Johann
What's-His-Name

PRESENTER: Beethoven, Mozart, Chopin, Liszt, Brahms, Schumann, Schubert, Mendelssohn and Bach. Names that will live forever. But there is one composer whose name is never included with the greats. Why is it that the world has never remembered the name of Johann Gambolputty de von Ausfernschpledenschlittcrasscrenbonfriedig-gerdingledangledonglebursteinvonknackerthrasherapplebanger-horowitzticolensicgranderknottyspelltinklegrandlichgrumblemeyer-spelterwasserkurstlichhimbleeisenbahnwagengutenabendbitteein-nürnburgerbratwurstlegerspurtemil zweimacheluberhundsfütgumbor-aberschönendankerkalbsfleischmittleraucher Von Hautkopft of Ulm?

To do justice to this man, thought by many to be the greatest name in German Baroque music, we present tonight a profile of Jo-hann Gambolputty de von Ausfernschpledenschlittcrasscrenbon-friediggerdingledangledonglebursteinvonknackerthrasherapple-bangerhorowitzticolensicgranderknottyspelltinklegrandlichgrumble-meyerspelterwasserkurstlichhimbleeisenbahnwagengutenabendbit-teeinürnburgerbratwurstlegerspurtenmitzweimacheluberhundsfüt-gumberaberschönendankerkalbsfleischmittleraucher von Hautkopft of Ulm. We start with an interview with his only surviving relative, his greatnephew, Karl, who is talking to Al Fry.

KARL: Oh ja. When I first met Johann Gambolputty de von Ausfernsch-pledenschlittcrasscrenbonfriediggerdingledangledongleburstein-vonknackerthrasherapplebangerhorowitzticolensicgranderknot-

tyspelltinklegrandlichgrumblemeyersp-
elterwasserkurstlichhimbleeisenbahn-
wagengutenabendbitteeinürnburgerbr-
atwurstlegerspurtenmitzweimachelub-
erhundsütgumberaberschönendanker-
kalbsfleischmittleraucher von Hautkopft
of Ulm, he was with his wife, Sarah
Gambolputty de von Ausfernschpledenschlittcrass...

INTERVIEWER: Yes, if I may just cut in on you there, Herr Gambolputty
de von Ausfernschpledenschlittcrasscrenbonfriediggerdingledan-
gledongleburrsteinvonknackerthrasherapplebangerhorowitzticolen-
sicgranderknottyspelltinklegrandlichgrumblemeyerspelterwasser-
kurstlichhimbleeisenbahnwagengutenabendbitteeinürnburgerbrat-
wurstlegerspurtenmitzweimacheluberhundsfütgumberaberschö-
nendankerkalbsfleischmittleraucher von Hautkopft of Ulm, and ask
you – just quickly – if there's any particular thing that you remember
about Johann Gambolputty de von Ausfernschpledenschlittcrass-
crenbonfriediggerdingledangledongleburrsteinvonknackerthrasher-
applebangerhorowitzticolensicgranderknottyspelltinklegrandlich-
grumblemeyerspelterwasserkurstlichhimbleeisenbahnwagenguten-
abendbitteeinürnburger-
bratwurstlegerspurten-
mitzweimacheluberhun-
dsfütgumberaberschö-
nendankerkalbsfleisch-
mittleraucher von Haut-
kopft of Ulm?
Hallo?

The Last Supper

POPE: Good evening, Michelangelo.

MICHELANGELO: Evening, your holiness.

POPE: I want to have a word with you about this 'Last Supper' of yours.

MICHELANGELO: Yes?

POPE: I'm not happy with it.

MICHELANGELO: Oh, dear. It took hours.

POPE: Not happy at all…

MICHELANGELO: Do the jellies worry you? They add a bit of colour, don't they? Oh, I know – you don't like the kangaroo.

POPE: … *What* kangaroo?

MICHELANGELO: I'll alter it, no sweat.

POPE: I never saw a kangaroo!

MICHELANGELO: It's right at the back, I'll paint it out, no problem. I'll make it into a disciple.

POPE: Ah!

MICHELANGELO: All right now?

POPE: That's the problem.

MICHELANGELO: … What is?

POPE: The disciples.

MICHELANGELO: Are they too Jewish? I made Judas the most Jewish.

POPE: No, no, it's just that there are twenty-eight of them.

MICHELANGELO: Well, another one would hardly notice, then.

POPE: No!!

MICHELANGELO: All right, all right, we'll lose the kangaroo altogether – I don't mind, I was never completely happy with it …

POPE: That's not the point. There are twenty-eight disciples.

MICHELANGELO: …Too many?

POPE: Of course it's too many!

MICHELANGELO: Well, in a way, but I wanted to give the impression of a huge get-together … you know, a real Last Supper – not any old supper, but a proper final treat…

POPE: There were only twelve disciples at the Last Supper.

MICHELANGELO: … Supposing some of the others happened to drop by?

POPE: There were only twelve altogether.

MICHELANGELO: Well, maybe they'd invited some friends?

POPE: There were only twelve disciples and Our Lord at the Last Supper. The Bible clearly says so.

MICHELANGELO: … No friends?

POPE: No friends.

MICHELANGELO: … Waiters?

POPE: No!

MICHELANGELO: … Cabaret?

POPE: No!!

MICHELANGELO: … You see, I like them. They fill out the canvas. I mean, I suppose we could lose three or four of them, you know, make them…

POPE: There were only twelve disciples and our Lord at the Last …

MICHELANGELO: I've got it, I've got it!!! We'll call it … 'The Penultimate Supper'. The Bible doesn't say how many people there were at that, does it?

POPE: Er, no, but …

MICHELANGELO: Well, there you are, then!

POPE: Look!! The Last Supper is a significant event in the life of

Our Lord. The Penultimate Supper was not, even if they had a conjurer and a steel band. Now I commissioned a Last Supper from you, and a Last Supper I want …

MICHELANGELO: Yes, but look …

POPE: … With twelve disciples and one Christ!

MICHELANGELO: … One?!

POPE: Yes, one. Now will you please tell me what in God's name possessed you to paint this with *three* Christs in it?

MICHELANGELO: It works, mate!!

POPE: It does not work!

MICHELANGELO: It does, it looks great! The fat one balances the two skinny ones!

POPE: There was only one Saviour …

MICHELANGELO: I know that, but what about a bit of artistic licence?

POPE: One Redeemer!

MICHELANGELO: I'll tell you what you want, mate, you want a bloody photographer, not a creative artist with some imagination!!

POPE: I'll tell you what I want – I want a Last Supper, with one Christ, twelve disciples, no kangaroos, by Thursday lunch, or you don't get paid!!

MICHELANGELO: You fascist!!

POPE: Look, I'm the bloody Pope I am!
I may not know much about art,
but I know what I like …

TOASTMASTER: Gentlemen, pray silence for the
President of the Royal Society for Putting Things
on Top of Other Things.

SIR WILLIAM: I thank you, gentlemen. The year
has been a good one for the Society

(*Cries of 'hear hear'*)

This year our members have put more things on
top of other things than ever before. But, I should
warn you, this is no time for complacency. No,
there are still many things, and I cannot emphasize
this too strongly, not on top of other things. I
myself, on my way here this evening, saw a thing
that was not on top of another thing in any way.

(*Cries of 'shame'*)

Shame indeed, but we must not allow ourselves to
become despondent. For we must never forget that
if there was not one thing that was not on top of
another thing, our society would be nothing more
than a meaningless body of men that had gathered
together for no good purpose. But we flourish.

This year our Australasian members and the
various organizations affiliated to our Australasian
branches put no fewer than twenty-two things on
top of other things.

(*Applause*)

Well done all of you. But there is one cloud on the
horizon. In this last year our Staffordshire branch
has not succeeded in putting one thing on top ...

(*and so on, and so on, and so on, and so on, and so on, and so on, and so on, and*

ARTHUR
'TWO SHEDS' JACKSON

INTERVIEWER: Last week the Royal Festival Hall saw the first performance of a new symphony by one of the world's leading modern composers, Arthur 'Two Sheds' Jackson. Mr Jackson, welcome.

JACKSON: Good evening.

INTERVIEWER: May I sidetrack you for one moment Mr Jackson, and ask about this nickname of yours.

JACKSON: Oh yes.

INTERVIEWER: 'Two Sheds'. How did you come by it?

JACKSON: Well I don't use it myself, it's just a few of my friends call me 'Two Sheds'.

INTERVIEWER: I see, and do you in fact have two sheds?

JACKSON: No. No, I've only one shed. I've had one for some time, but a few years ago I said I was thinking of getting another one and since then some people have called me 'Two Sheds'.

INTERVIEWER: In spite of the fact that you have only one.

JACKSON: Exactly.

INTERVIEWER: I see. And are you still thinking of purchasing a second shed?

JACKSON: No.

INTERVIEWER: I see, I see. Well let's return to your symphony. Now did you write this symphony ... *in* your shed?

JACKSON: ...No!

INTERVIEWER: Have you written any of your recent works in this shed of yours?

JACKSON: No. It's an ordinary garden shed.

INTERVIEWER: So were you thinking of buying this second shed to write in?

JACKSON: No, look, this shed business, it doesn't really matter at all, the sheds aren't important. It's just a few friends call me 'Two Sheds', and that's all there is to it. I wish you'd ask me about my music. People always ask me about the sheds, they've got it out of proportion, I'm fed up with the shed, I wish I'd never got it in the first place.

INTERVIEWER: Are you thinking of selling it?

JACKSON: Yes.

INTERVIEWER: Then you'd be Arthur 'No Sheds' Jackson!

JACKSON: Look, forget about the sheds! They don't matter!!!

Enter SECOND INTERVIEWER

SECOND INTERVIEWER: Are you having any trouble from him?

INTERVIEWER: A little.

SECOND INTERVIEWER: Well, we interviewers are more than a match for the likes of you, 'Two Sheds'.

INTERVIEWER: Yes make yourself scarce, 'Two Sheds'! This studio isn't big enough for the three of us.

SECOND INTERVIEWER: Get your own arts programme, you fairy!

WORD ASSOCIATION FOOTBALL

GOOD EVENING. TONIGHT'S THE NIGHT I SHALL BE TALKING ABOUT OF 'FLU THE SUBJECT OF WORD ASSOCIATION FOOTBALL. THIS IS A TECHNIQUE OUT A LIVING MUCH USED IN THE PRACTICE MAKES PERFECT OF PSYCHOANALYSISTER AND BROTHER AND ONE THAT HAS OCCUPIED PIPER THE MAJORITY RULE OF MY ATTENTION SQUAD BY THE RIGHT NUMBER ONE TWO THREE FOUR THE LAST FIVE YEARS TO THE MEMORY. IT IS QUITE REMARKABLEBAKERCHARLIE HOW MUCH THE MILLER'S SON THIS SO-CALLED WHILE YOU WERE OUT WORD ASSOCIATION IMMIGRANTS' PROBLEMS INFLUENCES THE MANNER FROM HEAVEN IN WHICH WE SLEEKIT COWERIN' TIMROUS BEASTIES ALL-AMERICAN SPEKE THE FAMOUS EXPLORER. AND THE REALLY WELL THAT IS SURPRISING PARTNER IN CRIME IS THAT A LOT AND HIS WIFE OF THE LIONS' FEEDINGTIME WE MAY BE C D E EFFECTIVELY QUITE UNAWARE OF THE FACT OR FICTION SECTION OF THE WATFORD PUBLIC LIBRARY THAT WE ARE EVEN DOING IT IS A FAR, FAR BETTER THING THAT I DO NOW THEN, NOW THEN, WHAT'S GOING ONWARD CHRISTIAN BARNARD THE FAMOUS HEARTY PART OF THE LETTUCE NOW PRAISE FAMOUS MENTAL HOMES FOR LOONIES LIKE ME. SO MY CONTENTION CAUSING ALL THE HEADACHES, IS THAT UNLESS WE TAKE INTO ACCOUNT OF MONTE-CRISTO IN OUR THINKING GEORGE V THIS PHENOMENON THE OTHER HAND WE SHALL NOT BE ABLE SATISFACT OR FICTIONSECTION OF THE WATFORD PUBLIC LIBRARYAGAINILY TO UNDERSTAND TO ATTENTION WHEN I'M TALKING TO YOU AND STOP LAUGHING, ABOUT HUMAN NATURE, MAN'S PSYCHOLOGICAL MAKE-UP SOME STORY THE WIFE'LL BELIEVE AND HENCE THE VERY MEANING OF LIFE ITSELFISH BASTARD I'LL KICK HIM IN THE BALL'S POND ROAD

NORMAN HENDERSON'S DIARY

Edited by Eric Henderson

Norman Henderson began keeping a diary on March 21st 1956. He continued to write that diary every day without fail until the day he died. As he himself puts it in that first entry: 'I have decided to keep ... a personal record ... of my most intimate thoughts'. He undertook this mammoth task, as I remember he undertook most things in his life, simply and uncomplainingly. He lived in a time when much was happening at home and abroad, and his diary is interesting historically for the way in which it reflects one man's reaction to his times, *at the time*. In a diary there is no benefit from hindsight – this is its strength as much as its weakness and here everything is reflected in the way it seemed then, without the perspective of distance.

Eric Henderson, Leicester, 1971

HISTORICAL NOTE

1956 was indeed a 'year of change', the title Norman Henderson adopted at the beginning of his diary for that year. Perhaps the high water mark of old-style Conservative government, under Sir Anthony Eden, England was shortly to plunge into the new world of Macmillan in the wake of the mammoth upheavals of the world around. On the home front it was the year of Princess Margaret's Caribbean Tour and the State Visit of King Haakon of Norway. Monsieur P. Wertheimer's Lavandin won the Derby, England won the Ashes with fine victories at Headingly and Trent Bridge, and Cambridge won the Boat Race for the 56th time.

1956 A YEAR OF CHANGE

Wednesday March 21st

I have been reading a lot of Harold Nicholson recently and have decided to keep a diary. It will be a personal record of my daily actions and my most intimate thoughts. Since I know most of the leading figures of the day, my experience of them too, may be of interest when my grandchildren come to read this account of an ordinary man in mid-twentieth century England.

Breakfasted with Peter [Thorneycroft], Selwyn [Lloyd] and Nathaniel [Jackley] whom I had specially invited to meet the others. They were alarmed at first by his sudden movements but thought his Suez invasion plan a good one if only the French and Israelis would agree.

Later visited Harrods. Went to Food Hall and bought up every single prawn they had! My, how they scurried about when I demanded to see the stock rooms in case they had missed one! Then crammed them all in a taxi and told cabbie to deliver to J. B. Priestley. I know he likes them. Bumped into Queen Juliana in the Electrical Department, buying bulbs. She in top form and ate one! Then I chased her down escalator pretending we were loonies. What a good sport she is!

Lunch with Hailsham and – [Civil Servant]. Asked – why he didn't have a name. He said it was hereditary; also very useful for tax purposes. After lunch were joined by Marquis of Salisbury so went to St James's Park in our badger outfits and hid behind bushes jumping out at civil servants. What a stuffy lot they are! One had a heart attack and a policeman was called; so we had to bribe him.

Went to first night of Three Sisters at Haymarket with Daphne and the Astors. Sat behind Lord Brabazon and next to Duchess of Argyll. Rather slow third act so we [N.H. *and* D.H. - Ed.] went up on stage and ran about a bit, causing quite a stir. We stopped when Tchebutykin's big soliloquy came, though, and sat down by him so as not to spoil people's enjoyment. What a sad speech it is! When it was over, though, we were up again, pushing the characters over till they had to bring the curtain down.

Went on to first night party afterwards. People seemed a little cool and the German ambassador scowled at us. Fucking Kraut. Who won the war? Felt rather depressed so stuffed pâté up my nose which cheered me up a lot. Then Queen Soraya arrived and I sneezed at worst possible moment. Then threw up over Duke of Norfolk. What a day! Went home and early bed but heard on news that Italy had annexed Yugoslavia. Later transpired it was a joke. Poor old BBC! Nothing they do is right.

Thursday March 22nd

Woke up late and read our reviews. Rather mixed.

At breakfast I had an innermost thought. How would horses run if they only had two legs, one at each end? A sort of rumba I suppose. Depressed me all morning.

Lunched with Duncan [Sandys], Heathcoat [Amory] and Reggie [Maudling] at Beefsteak. Duncan says Tony Chatsworth [Minister of Defence] is finished and must go [T.C. had at this point been dead for over four months - Ed.] Reggie agreed but said we must wait till after bye-elections [Nov 14th].

3 o'clock. Cabinet meeting. P.M. not looking at all well. Pale and drawn and wearing cork hat. Also cries a lot. Asked me what I thought about cheese. What could I say? I replied that it was reliable enough stuff but that he should not count on it in an emergency. He seemed satisfied by this but Barbara [Windsor] thought it v. funny. She is a nice enough lady but must be a risk at the Board of Trade. Eventually meeting finished. Sad to see PM

in this state. Just yodels to himself and makes faces in mirror. Also incontinent. And yet he is the best man we have! I was also surprised to find how easy it had been to get into a cabinet meeting. A lot of foreigners there too.

Met Harold [Macmillan] and Lady Violet [Bonham-Carter] at Moo-Cow in Greek Street. Harold said crisis was on us but felt it best to keep it from nation in case they got annoyed. Baited waitress.

Tea at the Menuhins. A lot of fighting as usual. Took taxi home in nude but was involved in an accident with a lorry in Oxford Street. Was quite badly hurt and had to travel in ambulance to hospital. Died before we got there, though.

Friday March 23rd

Nothing much. Funeral arranged for tomorrow. Rather depressed.

Saturday March 24th

Service at St Thomas, Belgravia.
Then on to cemetery.
Buried about 11.15 a.m.

KING ARTHUR AND HIS KNIGHTS ARE OVERJOYED TO REACH THE CASTLE.

The Sacred Castle

SUDDENLY A VOICE COMES FROM THE BATTLEMENTS...

FROG: Hello smelly English kerniggets ... and Monsieur Arthur King, who has the brain of a duck, y'know. We French persons outwit you a second time, perfidious English mousedropping hoarders, begorrah!

ARTHUR: How dare you profane this place with your presence! I command you, in the name of the Knights of Camelot, open the door to the Sacred Castle to which God himself has guided us!

FROG: How you English say, I one more time, mac, unclog my nose towards you, sons of a window-dresser! So you think you could out-clever us French fellows with your silly knees-bent creeping about advancing behaviour. I wave my private parts at your aunties, you brightly-coloured, cranberry-smelling, electric donkey-bottom biters.

ARTHUR: In the name of our Lord, we demand entrance to the Sacred Castle.

FROG: No chance, English bed-wetting types. We burst our pimples at you, and call your door-opening request a silly thing. You tiny-brained wipers of other people's bottoms.

Much French laughter.

ARTHUR: If you do not open these doors, we will take the castle by force ...

A bucket of what can only be described as human waste hits ARTHUR, ARTHUR leads the knights away. French jeering follows them.

FROG: Yes, depart a lot at this time, and cut the approaching any more or we fire arrows into the tops of your heads and make castanets of your testicles already. Your mother was a hamster and your father smelt of elderberries.

ARTHUR (*to KNIGHTS*). Just ignore him.

A small hail of chickens, watercress, badgers and mattresses lands on them.

FROG: And now remain gone, illegitimate-faced bugger-folk! And if you think you got a nasty taunting this time, you ain't heard nothing yet, dappy kerniggets and A.King Esquire.

SPOT THE SPECIES

A.

B.

C.

D.

E.

F.

G.

H.

I.

A. RED-RUFFED LEMUR
B. MOUSE LEMUR
C. WHITE-FRONTED LEMUR
D. RING-TAILED LEMUR
E. COQUEREL'S SIFAKA
F. HURLEY'S LEMUR
G. GENTLE LEMUR
H. DWARF LEMUR
I. MONGOOSE LEMUR

DOCUMENTARY

MRS JALIN: There's a man at the door.
MR JALIN: What's he want?
MRS JALIN: He says do we want a documentary on molluscs.
MR JALIN: What's he mean, molluscs?
MRS JALIN: MOLLUSCS!! GASTROPODS! LAMELLIBRANCHS! CEPHALOPODS!
MR JALIN: Oh, molluscs. What's he charge then?
MRS JALIN: It's free.
MR JALIN: Ooh! Where does he want us to sit?

ZORBA: Good morning. Tonight molluscs. The mollusc is a soft-bodied, unsegmented invertebrate animal usually protected by a large shell. One of the most numerous groups of invertebrates, it is exceeded in number of species only by the arthropods viz, this lobster.

MRS JALIN: Not very interesting is it?

ZORBA: What?

MRS JALIN: I was talking to my husband.

ZORBA: Oh. Anyway, the typical mollusc, viz, this snail, consists of a prominent muscular portion, the head-foot, a visceral mass and a shell which is secreted by the free edge of the mantle.

MRS JALIN: Dreadful isn't it?

ZORBA: ... What?

MRS JALIN: I was talking to him.

ZORBA: Oh. Well anyway ... in some molluscs, however, viz, this slug, the shell is absent or rudimentary ...

MR JALIN: Switch him off.

MRS JALIN *gets up and looks for the switch.*

ZORBA: Whereas in others, viz, cephalopods, the head-foot is greatly modified and forms tentacles, viz, the squid. What are you doing?

MRS JALIN: Switching you off.

ZORBA: Why, don't you like it?

MRS JALIN: Oh it's dreadful.

MR JALIN: Embarrassing.

ZORBA: ...Is it?

MR JALIN: I don't know how they've got the nerve to put it on.

MRS JALIN: It's so boring.

ZORBA: Well, it's not much of a subject is it? Be fair.

MRS JALIN: What do you think, George?

MR JALIN: Give him another twenty seconds.

ZORBA: Anyway the majority of the molluscs are included in three large groups , the gastropods, the lamellibranchs and the cephalopods.

MRS JALIN: We *know* that.

MR JALIN: Switch him off!

ZORBA: However, what is more interesting, is the mollusc's sex life.

MRS JALIN : ... Oh!

ZORBA: Yes, the mollusc is a randy little fellow whose primitive brain scarcely strays from the subject of you-know-what.

MRS JALIN : Disgusting!

ZORBA : The randiest of the gastro-pods is the limpet. This hot-blooded little beast with its tent-like shell is always on the job. Its extra-marital activities are something startling. Frankly I don't know how the female limpet finds the time to adhere to the rock-face. How am I doing?

MRS JALIN: It's disgusting.

MR JALIN: But more interesting.

MRS JALIN: Oh yes. Tch, tch, tch, tch, tch, tch.

ZORBA: Another loose-living gastropod is the periwinkle. This shameless little libertine with its characteristic ventral locomotion is not the marrying kind. 'Anywhere, anytime' is its motto. Up with the shell and they're at it.

MRS JALIN: How about the lamellibranchs?

ZORBA: I'm coming to them. Take the scallop This tatty, scrofulous old rapist, is second in depravity only to the common clam. This latter is a right whore, a harlot, a trollop, a cynical bed-hopping firm-breasted Rabelaisian bit of sea food that makes Fanny Hill look like a dead pope. And finally among the bivalves, that most depraved of the whole sub-species – the whelk. The whelk is nothing but a homosexual of the worst kind. This gay boy of the gastropods, this queer crustacean, this mincing mollusc, this screaming, prancing, limp-wristed queen of the deep makes me sick.

MRS JALIN: Have you got one?

ZORBA: Here!

MRS JALIN: Let's kill it.

ZORBA *throws it on the floor and Mr and Mrs Jalin stamp on it.*

MR JALIN: That'll teach it. Well thank you for a very interesting programme.

ZORBA: Oh, not at all. Thank you.

MRS JALIN: Yes, that was very nice.

ZORBA: Thank you.

MR JALIN: Thank *you*.

Chapel

HEADMASTER: And spotteth twice they the camels before the third hour. And so the Midianites went forth to Ram Gilead in Kadesh Bilgemath by Shor Ethra Regalion, to the house of Gash-Bil-Bethuel-Bazda, he who brought the butter dish to Balshazar and the tent peg to the house of Rashomon, and there slew they the goats, yea, and placed they the bits in little pots.
Here endeth the lesson.

CHAPLAIN: Let us praise God. Oh Lord ...
CONGREGATION: Oh Lord ...
CHAPLAIN: Oooh, you are so big ...
CONGREGATION: Oooh, you are so big ...
CHAPLAIN: So absolutely *huge*.
CONGREGATION: So absolutely *huge*.
CHAPLAIN: Gosh, we're all really impressed down here I can tell you.
CONGREGATION: Hear hear!
CHAPLAIN: Forgive us, oh Lord, for this our dreadful toadying.
CONGREGATION: And barefaced flattery.
CHAPLAIN: But you are so strong and, well, just so *super*.
CONGREGATION: Fan-*tastic*!
HEADMASTER: Amen. Now two boys have been found rubbing linseed oil into the school cormorant. Now some of you may feel that the cormorant does not play an important part in the life of the school but would remind you that it was presented to us by the Corporation of the town of Sudbury to commemorate Empire Day, when we try to

remember the names of all those from the Sudbury area who so gallantly gave their lives to keep China British. So from now on the cormorant is strictly out of bounds. And Jenkins, apparently your mother died this morning.

Oh Lord, please don't burn us,
Don't grill or toast your flock.
Don't put us on the barbecue,
Or simmer us in stock.
Don't braise or bake or boil us,
Or stir-fry us in a wok ...

Oh please don't lightly poach us,
Or baste us with hot fat.
Don't fricassée or roast us,
Or boil us in a vat.
And please don't stick thy servants Lord,
In a Rotissomat ...

INDEX